Praise for WILL IT BLOW?

"Elizabeth Rusch's humor-spiced *Will It Blow?* takes youngsters on a geologic adventure that both entertains and informs. Though aimed at younger readers, adults also will delight in learning more about volcanoes and the scientists who study them in this witty, engaging book."
—RICHARD HILL, SCIENCE WRITER, *The Oregonian*

"Part comic book, part scrapbook, part puzzle book, *Will It Blow?* is so much fun that kids won't even realize how much they're learning. This book should be *legally* required for all kids studying geology."
—KRISTIN HOSTETTER, GEAR EDITOR, *Backpacker Magazine*

"Your mission, should you choose to accept it: Read this fabulous book! *Will It Blow?* enlists readers in the 'Department of Volcanic Investigation' and sends them off to infiltrate the scientific mysteries of Mount St. Helens. Along the way they'll be debriefed by experts and have a chance to sharpen their sleuthing skills as they learn how to decode the clues that could help predict the next eruption of one of North America's most active volcanoes. Double-oh-fun for aspiring volcano detectives of any age."
—HEATHER VOGEL FREDERICK, AUTHOR OF THE POPULAR *Spy Mice* SERIES

"*Will it Blow?* captures the excitement and urgency of vulcanology and the hands-on challenges of the science. Rusch doesn't gloss over the uncertainty and confusion geologists face as they try to figure out what's going on miles below the surface and what it might mean to people who live near a volcano. Let's hope it inspires a new generation of geologists to learn more about what makes volcanoes tick and how to better predict when the ticking bomb is about to go off."
—SANDI DOUGHTON, SCIENCE REPORTER, *The Seattle Times*

"What do M&Ms, gophers, and soda straws have in common? They're all clever analogies author Elizabeth Rusch uses to explain the inner workings of nature's smokestacks. What an enjoyable and informative book! Even after covering volcanoes for many years, I learned something."
—ANDRE STEPANKOWSKY, *The Daily News*,
WINNER OF A PULITZER FOR COVERAGE OF MOUNT ST. HELENS' 1980 ERUPTION

WILL IT

Become a Volcano Detective at Mount St. Helens

ELIZABETH RUSCH *illustrated by* K.E. LEWIS

SASQUATCH BOOKS
SEATTLE

For Cobi

Note: The volcano warning system of the Cascades Volcano Observatory in 2004 used level one, two, and three instead of advisory, watch, and warning. The observatory adopted the nationwide alert system in 2006.

Printed in China

Published by Sasquatch Books
Distributed by Publishers Group West
15 14 13 12 11 10 09 08 07   9 8 7 6 5 4 3 2 1

Design by Kate Basart / Union Pageworks
Photos of Mount St. Helens by various staff of the United States Geological Survey.

Library of Congress Cataloging-in-Publication Data is available.

ISBN: 1-57061-510-1 (hardcover) / 1-57061-509-8 (paperback)

Sasquatch Books / 119 South Main Street, Suite 400 / Seattle, WA 98104
206.467.4300 / www.sasquatchbooks.com / custserv@sasquatchbooks.com

CONTENTS

YOUR MISSION

Your mission, if you choose to accept it, is to predict a Mount St. Helens eruption. It's not enough to catch Mount St. Helens red-handed. To protect the public, you must sniff out what kind of volcanic trouble is brewing. Will the volcano shoot ash high into the air? Will hot lava melt the icy glacier, unleashing a deadly mudflow? Or will Mount St. Helens just blow off a little steam and quiet down again?

THE STAKES: This mission is critical. Every year, hundreds of thousands of people visit Johnston Ridge, just five miles from the summit. Are tourists in danger of being pelted with pumice? Hikers and backpackers romp on the trails all around the volcano, even climbing up to the crater rim. Will they be blasted by blistering volcanic gases? Airplanes and helicopters regularly fly over Mount St. Helens. Will volcanic ash clog their engines? Houses and cabins dot the valley. Could they be swept away by a mudflow?

THE CLUES: It takes *real* detective work to answer these questions. Like all volcanoes, Mount St. Helens leaves clues. Not fingerprints or footprints, but earthquakes, gases and other clues that can help you guess what the volcano might do next.

THE CASES: After you've been trained to decipher these volcanic clues, you can put your detective skills to the test with real life cases from Mount St. Helens. Crack these cases and you'll be ready to predict volcanic eruptions anywhere in the world!

Do you accept the mission? It's time for your first briefing.

THE SUSPECT

NAME: Mount St. Helens

ALIASES: Louwala Clough, Loo-Wit Lat-kla, Smoking Mountain

AGE: 300,000 years

RESIDENCE: Southwest Washington, U.S.A.

HEIGHT: 8,364 feet (9,677 feet before May 18, 1980)

DESCRIPTION: The youngest and most active of a gang of volcanoes called the Cascades, this suspect is part of a large volcanic operation known as the Ring of Fire. Most of the world's active volcanoes belong to the Ring of Fire, a chain that circles the Pacific Ocean.

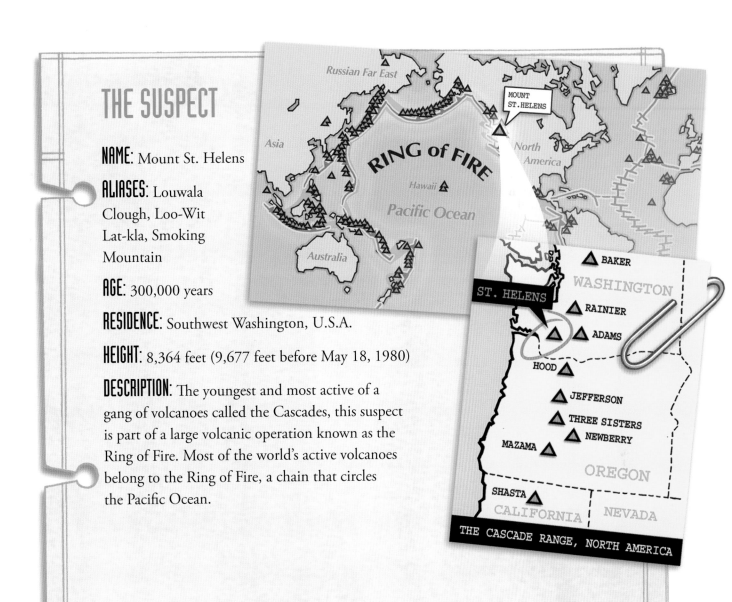

How is the Earth Like a Peanut M&M?

Because it's crunchy and chocolaty when you bite into it? No! Because it has three layers, just like a peanut M&M. The crust, like the crunchy candy coating of the M&M, is a shell of solid rock. The mantle is like the soft chocolate, with rock so hot that it melts into thick paste. The core is like the peanut, solid metal in the center of the earth.

The Earth is not exactly like a peanut M&M, though. The crust is not all one piece. It's broken up into huge slabs, called plates, that cover the Earth like a jigsaw puzzle. These plates move apart and crash together all over the place.

Along the edge of the Pacific Ocean, plates collide, forming the Ring of Fire. Where one plate is forced under another plate, pressure and heat melt the rock. The melted rock rises through cracks, or vents, to the Earth's surface. If the magma rises high enough it can erupt, like at Mount St. Helens. Watch out!

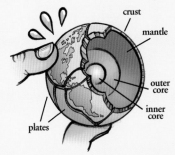

Known Hideouts

Aboveground, Mount St. Helens looks like an upside down ice cream cone, with the point snapped off. It's basically made of layers of ash and lava. Most of Mount St. Helens' volcanic activity happens underground, a hideout that no detective can penetrate. In fact, no one knows what Mount St. Helens looks like beneath the Earth's surface.

But detectives have a theory. They think the middle of Mount St. Helens is like a soda straw hundreds of feet wide. This giant tube is a vent that leads five to ten miles down into the Earth. Somewhere down there is a huge area of melted and partially melted rock and gases, called magma. This magma can bubble—or explode—to the surface at any time.

EXTERIOR:

INTERIOR:

1mi
2mi
3mi
4mi
5mi
6mi
7mi
8mi
9mi
10mi
11mi
12mi

vent

MAGMA

Prior Offenses

Mount St. Helens is one to watch closely, folks. The suspect has a long history of eruptions. Mount St. Helens has:

 Spit steam

 Blown its top, spewing ash, rocks, and gas into the atmosphere

 Leaked red, runny lava

 Buried everything nearby in ash and rock puffed up with gas (called pumice)

 Hurled rocks

 Scorched the area with searing hot gas and ash (called pyroclastic flows)

 Launched massive landslides

 Dragged trees, cabins, and elk for miles in thick rivers of mud called mudflows or lahars.

Disguises

Mount St. Helens is a master of deception, disguised for long periods of time as an inactive, or dormant, volcano. In 1980, the volcano had a perfect cone shape with a majestic snow-capped peak. On its peaceful flanks, lush green forests teemed with wildlife. In its valleys, clear mountain lakes shimmered with fish. All around, cabins, camps, and trails bustled with people. Mount St. Helens had everyone fooled—for more than 100 years.

Master of Disguises
Mount St. Helens through the Ages

HEY, WHERE'S THE VOLCANO?

500,000 to 300,000 years ago
Before Mount St. Helens, the area had only low, jagged hills.

ONE VOLCANO, TWO VOLCANOES, THREE VOLCANOES, FOUR

300,000 to 35,000 years ago
Multiple vents occasionally spew ash to make a bunch of domes.

NOW YOU SEE IT, NOW YOU DON'T

28,000 to 17,000 years ago
A huge avalanche flattens the volcano.

A SERIOUS GROWTH SPURT

16,000 to 13,000 years ago
Lava domes rebuild the summit to nearly 7,000 feet.

KA-BAM!

4,000 to 2,500 years ago
The largest known explosive eruption hurls ash, lava, and gases.

WHAT A CONEHEAD!

2,500 to 1,900 years ago
Hot, runny lava covers the domes and makes an 8,500-foot high cone.

IT KEEPS GROWING AND GROWING

1479 to 1857
Eruptions add 1,000 feet and build small domes. Zzzz, Mount St. Helens goes dormant.

WHAMMO!

1980 to 1986
The landslide of May 1980 rips 1,300 feet off the summit. In a few years, gooey lava erupts and hardens, creating a dome. Then the volcano nods off. Nightie, night.

Recent Violent Activity

On March 20, 1980, volcano detectives caught Mount St. Helens red-handed—shaking the area with a 4.2 magnitude earthquake. Hundreds of small earthquakes followed. A week later, steam and ash exploded from the snowy peak, blasting a hole, or crater, that grew to more than 1,000 feet wide.

Detectives then discovered a huge bulge on the north side of the volcano. They had a hunch that magma pooling underground was swelling the volcano, like a massive bump on your head. But this bump was growing five or six feet a day! By mid-May, the bulge was a half mile wide, a mile long, and 300 feet high—as high as an eighteen-story building.

Fearing an eruption, officials banned commercial airplanes from flying overhead. They told people nearby to leave their homes. Everyone expected something to happen, but no one knew exactly what the suspect would do.

  THEN, AT 8:32 A.M. on May 18, 1980, Mount St. Helens struck again with a big 5.1 earthquake.

THE QUAKE LOOSENED THE MASSIVE BULGE, which slid and tore off the entire top and north side of the mountain. It was the biggest landslide in recorded history! Moving faster than the world's fastest roller coaster, the landslide buried twenty-four square miles—an area the size of Manhattan—under 150 feet of earth and rocks.

THE TOP OF THE MOUNTAIN SLIDING OFF was like a cork popping off a champagne bottle. Gases and magma trapped underground ripped through the landslide. The explosion, called a "stone wind," blasted ash, rocks, even boulders sideways at speeds of up to 730 miles per hour. That's faster than the speed of sound!

THEN THE VOLCANO BEGAN ERUPTING UPWARD. For nine hours, it hurtled a dark column of ash and gas fifteen miles into the air. That's twice as high as most airplanes fly! Wind blew millions of tons of ash across the United States, causing complete darkness at noon in Spokane, Washington, a four-hour drive away. Eventually the ash-cloud circled the entire globe.

GAS, ASH, AND PUMICE rolled down the volcano's sides. These pyroclastic flows were more than 1,000°F—hot enough to melt your shoes.

THE HEAT OF THE ERUPTION MELTED HEAPS OF ICE AND SNOW. The melted water mixed together with ash, rock, and dirt into a big gooey mess as thick as concrete. Huge masses of mud flowed down the valley, tearing out bridges, ripping up houses, and smothering fish and other animals.

At the end of the day, Mount St. Helens was 1,300 feet shorter, with a gaping horseshoe-shaped crater more than two miles long, a mile wide, and 2,000 feet deep. Fifty-seven people died in the eruption. Two hundred homes were destroyed. Thousands of animals perished. In a single day, a pristine mountain landscape was transformed into a gray, steaming moonscape.

Recent Disguise

For six years after the 1980 eruption, Mount St. Helens dabbled in petty crime, occasionally spewing gas, ash, and thick lava. The volcano began to rebuild itself. In seventeen small eruptions of stiff, thick lava, Mount St. Helens built a new dome inside the crater. The dome grew to almost 900 feet high. Then in 1986, the volcano slipped back into its disguise as a dormant volcano.

But Mount St. Helens may have set a trap. Like a pea stuck in a soda straw, cooled magma may have plugged up the top mile of the vent. If pressure builds, that mile-long cork could blow . . .

chapter 1
EARTHQUAKE CLUES

Now that you've been briefed on the suspect, it's time to learn what it takes to be a volcano sleuth. Five real detectives from the Cascades Volcano Observatory in Vancouver, Washington, agreed to take their eyes off the sneaky volcano just long enough to train you as a private eye. Here now is Seth Moran, a detective specializing in earthquakes, to put you hot on the trail of the first clue.

SHAKE, RATTLE, AND ROLL

Seth wishes he had a huge X-ray machine that would allow him to watch what goes on inside Mount St. Helens. Or a robot that could tunnel down and not get fried. Or a huge chainsaw to cut the volcano in half so he could see what's happening inside. But all he has to work with for now is a seismograph, a special tool that measures earthquakes.

"Earthquakes are often the very first clue that a volcano is waking up," says Seth. As magma rises, it pushes and breaks rock, literally shaking the ground with its power. The seismograph moves with the ground when it shakes and records the movement. The squiggly line it makes is called a seismogram.

Singing Seismograph

GADGETS & GIZMOS

Did you know that quaking volcanoes can make music? In the old days, seismographs were made with a pencil attached to a spring. When earthquakes made the spring move, the pencil recorded the movement. The only sound you could hear was a scratch, scratch.

Today, the principle of a seismograph is the same, but a magnet and coil have replaced the pencil. Instead of drawing a line, the moving magnet generates electricity. The electricity is translated into a tone, which can be seen (as a wavy line on a seismogram) and heard! "Each seismograph sings its own tune," Seth Moran says. So when the earth quakes under Mount St. Helens, the seismographs literally sing: "Wee-ah, wee-ah, wee-ah!"

"Just detecting one earthquake doesn't tell you enough," says Seth. It's like finding a fingerprint at a crime scene. You have to learn more about it.

COUNT THE QUAKES

The first clue earthquake detectives look for is simple: A big jump in the number of earthquakes. When Mount St. Helens is dormant, one earthquake a day is normal. But if scientists see an earthquake or two every hour, that's a clue that something's afoot.

A bunch of earthquakes one right after another is called a swarm. And a swarm could lead to an eruption. "Of course, swarms sometimes don't lead to anything, no eruption, nothing," Seth admits. So how do you tell the difference between a swarm that leads to an eruption and one that doesn't? It's elementary, my dear Watson.

LOCATION, LOCATION, LOCATION!

First, pinpoint the location of the earthquake. Is it under the volcano? If not, it's probably not volcanic. If it *is* under the volcano, how deep is it?

Shallow earthquakes, a mile or less underground, could mean magma is bulldozing its way through the plug toward the surface. The volcano could blow.

Deeper earthquakes signal that magma is moving deep within the earth. If the earthquakes stay deep—below two miles—no need to worry. But if that deep magma nears the surface, stand back! Deeper magma, which is under pressure and holds explosive gases, can be much more dangerous. "Swarms up and down the vent would have us really concerned," Seth says. "That would mean magma was pounding its way to the surface from deep below—that would be intense."

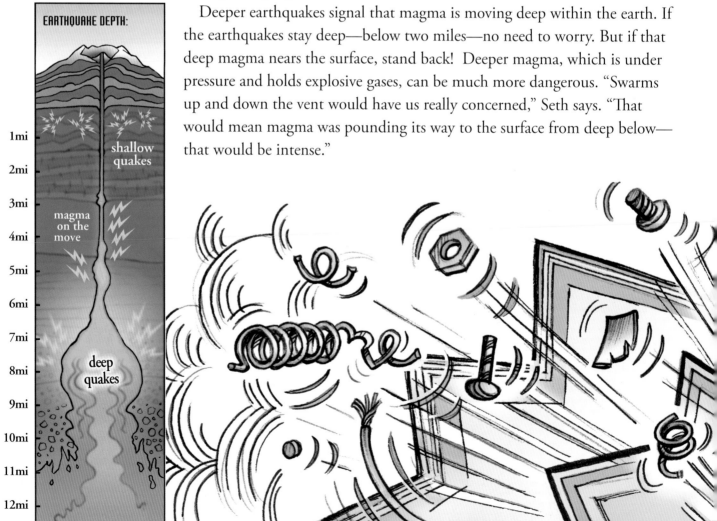

EARTHQUAKE DEPTH:

1mi

shallow quakes

2mi

3mi

magma on the move

4mi

5mi

6mi

7mi

deep quakes

8mi

9mi

10mi

11mi

12mi

SIZE MATTERS

The size of an earthquake at certain volcanoes can hint at the size of an eruption. After studying seismograms, scientists assign numbers to show the power of an earthquake. Magnitude 1, 2, or 3 quakes at Mount St. Helens suggest that a smaller eruption might be coming. Magnitude 4 or 5 quakes suggest that large amounts of volcanic gases and melted rock are pushing through large sections of the volcano. If it blows, it could be big.

MAKE A MATCH

Like analyzing a fingerprint, volcano detectives compare new seismograms with ones from the past, looking for the perfect match. Does the seismogram have a few narrow, tall spikes close together or waves that are more spread out?

A classic clue: a seismogram with the wiggles moving slowly up and down. "We think it's magma and gas pulsing in a crack," Seth explains.

Even more worrisome than a slow, wavy seismogram is a constant shaking of the ground, called a harmonic tremor. Harmonic tremors, which can last from ten minutes to several days, often warn that magma is really on the move.

THE BEST CLUE: KA-BOOM!

The final clue is a flat line on the seismogram, which means the machine is busted. In the 1980 eruption, all the seismographs on the mountain were blown to smithereens. "When you lose your stations, that's a big clue that something's going on," Seth says. "The problem is, you only get that clue once!"

Real Mount St. Helens Seismograms

Normal background activity when dormant:

A helicopter on the ground:

Earthquakes that didn't lead to an eruption:

Earthquakes that led to an eruption:

HARMONIC TREMOR:

Steam explosion:

Blown-up seismograph:

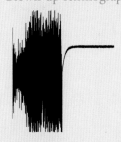

Human Seismograph

Lie on your belly in the center of the bed, perpendicular to the wall, with your arm straight and your fingertips touching the wall. Get two of your friends to stand beside the bed, one to the left of you, one to the right. Now, have these two friends hold the long white paper against the wall so that you're touching the paper with your fingertips. Place the pencil in your hand so that its point is pressed firmly against the paper.

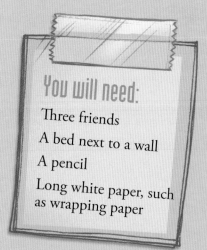

You will need:
Three friends
A bed next to a wall
A pencil
Long white paper, such as wrapping paper

1. Have your friends pull the paper slowly from left to right. What kind of line did you make?

2. Ask your third friend to hit the bed far from you and near you. What shape is the line now?

3. Now ask the same friend to sit down hard on the bed and then bounce. What shape is the line now? How can you and your friends make lines with different shapes?

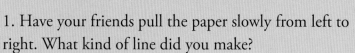

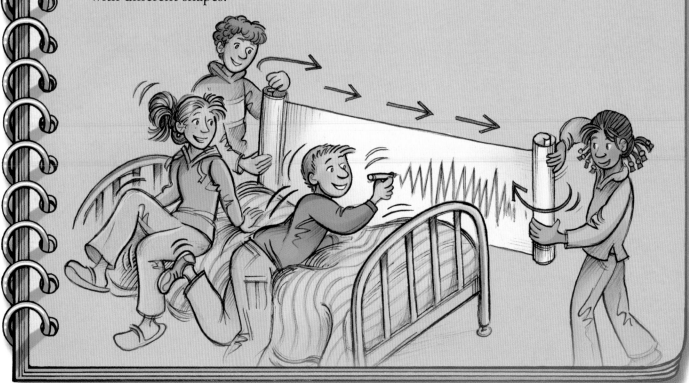

THE MYSTERY OF THE EARTHQUAKE SWARMS

Your first case begins 18 years after Mount St. Helens went dormant.

At 2:00 A.M. on September 23, 2004, while the volcano detectives slept, earthquakes rumbled under Mount St. Helens. When Seth Moran got to work that morning, he checked the seismograms from the night before. He was shocked. The seismographs had detected one earthquake an hour, then two an hour, then ten or twenty earthquakes an hour! "When earthquakes start stacking up, they get your attention fast," he says.

Right away Seth popped his head into the office of Cynthia Gardner, the acting scientist-in-charge. "Just a heads up," he said, "We've got a little earthquake swarm."

"Oh! Really?" she said. "Watch it closely."

That day, seismographs recorded more than 200 small earthquakes, all less than magnitude 1.0. They were located about a half-mile below the lava dome created in 1986.

"Could this develop into something serious?" Cynthia asked her colleagues.

"Let me do some research," Seth replied. Seth compared the day's seismograms with those from Mount St. Helens' past. The last swarm with a couple of hundred earthquakes in a day occurred in November 2001. The vast majority of these were less than magnitude 1.0, and they were shallower. The seismograms from that swarm looked like Figure One.

That swarm petered out to nothing.

Mount St. Helens also rocked in 1998, when about ten earthquakes a day, mostly smaller than magnitude 2.0, rumbled six miles below. They looked like Figure Two.

But the volcano didn't erupt then either.

Scientists debated the cause of the new quakes. One theory: water from heavy September rains was leaking into the volcano. When water hits hot rock, the rock can crack, causing earthquakes. But it was also possible that magma was charging to the surface.

The next day, earthquakes came fast, a few *every minute*. They looked like Figure Three.

At 10:00 A.M., scientists released an Information Statement, alerting the public. That day, Mount St. Helens had the most earthquakes in a day since 1983 and 1984—when it was erupting. The volcano detectives wondered:

Was Mount St. Helens rumbling back to life? Would the swarms continue and lead to an eruption or would they just disappear?

SEARCH FOR THESE CLUES

- ☐ Shallow earthquakes greater than magnitude 1.0
- ☐ More than one earthquake a day
- ☐ A seismogram that matches a slow earthquake—or a harmonic tremor!

Figure One

Figure Two

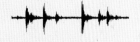

Figure Three

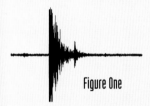

CASE CLOSED

Seth Moran concluded that the swarms most closely resembled the 2001 swarms that didn't lead to an eruption.

On Saturday, September 25, the earthquakes slowed down to about one per minute. "I've seen this before, swarms fizzling out to nothing," says Seth. "I really thought it was over."

He was wrong!

Later in the afternoon, Seth was home mowing his lawn when he got an urgent call. The earthquakes were getting bigger.

Seth hustled over to the observatory. He and his colleagues set up a night watch, waking every three hours to check the seismographs. Over the next twenty-four hours the earthquakes got bigger and bigger and more and more frequent. The earthquakes—some as large as magnitude 3.0—rocked the volcano every minute! They looked like Figure One.

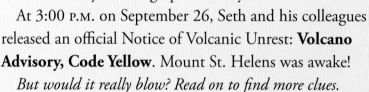

Figure One

"It was really building up!" Seth says.

At 3:00 P.M. on September 26, Seth and his colleagues released an official Notice of Volcanic Unrest: **Volcano Advisory, Code Yellow**. Mount St. Helens was awake!

But would it really blow? Read on to find more clues.

Danger, Danger! Mount St. Helens Alert Levels

A volcano can toss ash high into the sky, wreaking havoc on airplane engines without endangering people on the ground. And lava flows and mudflows can make a mess on the ground while skies remain clear. So how do volcano detectives warn about these different dangers? They use two alert systems. The nationwide volcano warning system uses three words you may have heard during weather alerts—advisory, watch, and warning. The international aviation alert system uses catchy color codes. Before you take a hike or helicopter ride near an active volcano, check out these alert levels:

ADVISORY	Unusual earthquakes or gas emissions suggest a volcano is awakening.
CODE YELLOW	An ash eruption is possible in the next few weeks.
WATCH	An explosion or eruption is possible, but not likely to hurt people or property on the ground. (Also used during ongoing harmless eruptions.)
CODE ORANGE	An eruption, with little or no ash, is possible within days.
WARNING	A dangerous explosion or eruption is likely—or underway.
CODE RED	A major eruption with large ash plumes is underway or expected within twenty-four hours.

chapter 2

GAS CLUES

PASSING GAS

Escaping gas? Sounds like an embarrassing incident after eating burritos, doesn't it? But it's actually the next volcanic clue. Once earthquakes reveal that a volcano is awake, gas detectives like Ken McGee rush to the scene.

On a typical gas mission, Ken straps gas detectors to the outside of a helicopter or airplane. "We orbit the inside of the crater looking for any trace of gas," he says.

MAGMA ON THE MOVE

Why search for gas clues? Imagine a bottle of soda that you've shaken but you haven't opened. It's full of gas ready to fizz out. But you don't see many bubbles because the gas is under pressure. Magma under the Earth is like the soda. It's a mixture of liquid (melted rock) and gas under high pressure.

As magma pushes up a volcano's vent, it's like that hiss you hear when you open a soda bottle. The pressure drops and some gas escapes. At a restless volcano, gas may escape in a slow leak at first. But when gassy magma nears the surface, the volcano can really pop.

"Expanding gas powers an eruption," says Ken. In other words, gas provides the force that can blast lava and ash out of a volcano. Ka-Pow!

SNIFFING OUT THE GAS

Volcano detectives sniff out three kinds of gas clues: carbon dioxide, hydrogen sulfide, and sulfur dioxide. "The more gas that comes out, the larger, more explosive the eruption can be," says Ken. "Big gas numbers usually mean you have a big pot of magma down there."

WAITING TO EXHALE

When magma moves underground, the first gas to sneak out is the same gas we exhale: carbon dioxide. More and more carbon dioxide will escape as magma gets closer and closer to the surface.

Carbon dioxide is odorless and invisible. So how the heck can you find it? Detectives suck air samples into a special tool that detects the gas. If a volcano has a steam plume, like a cloud rising from the vent, volcano detectives fly straight into it. A plume is a great place to scout for carbon dioxide.

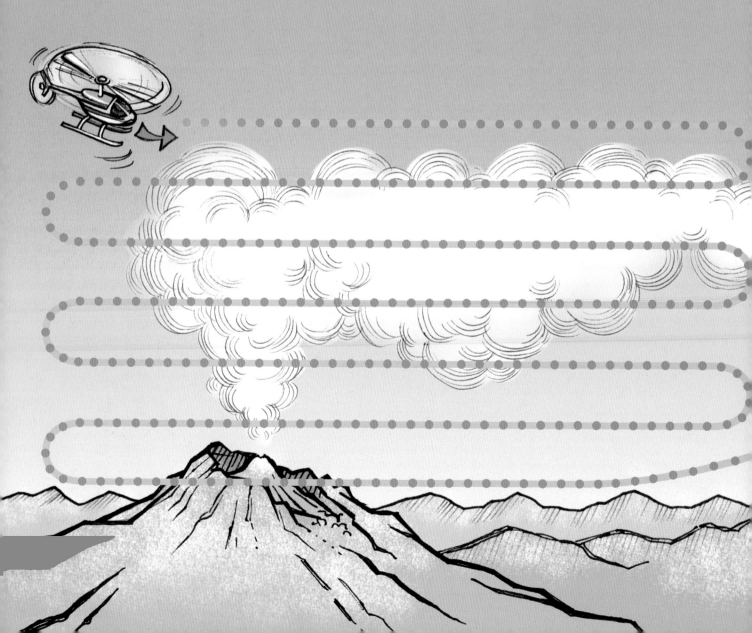

THE STINKY CLUES

Gas detectives also try to sniff out hydrogen sulfide. Really, they sniff. "The rotten-egg smell of hydrogen sulfide is a classic early warning that a volcano might blow," says Ken.

The last gas clue is stinky one, too. "Sulfur dioxide has an acrid, acidy smell—a burning taste almost," Ken says. "It's nasty." If the stench of sulfur dioxide isn't enough to scare you away, what it signals will. "When you detect sulfur dioxide, you know the volcano has heated up and that magma is really close to erupting," says Ken.

To search for a surge in sulfur dioxide, detectives must fly under a plume, so their instruments can look up into the steam and gas above. This is harder than it sounds. "If the winds are very high, the plume gets pushed down the flank of the volcano and you struggle to get underneath it without hitting the slope," says Ken. A helicopter or plane hitting a crater wall is not a good thing.

"It's scary when the winds are high," says Ken. "It's like riding a bucking bronco. You get buffeted around, up and down—it's crazy." But it's all in a day's detective work.

Catch Some Rays!

GADGETS & GIZMOS

To measure sulfur dioxide, volcano detectives use a cool tool called FLYSPEC. It's a tiny box, just three inches by three inches.

Here's how FLYSPEC works. You know how your sunglasses block burning ultraviolet rays? Well, sulfur dioxide blocks a specific ray of light, too. The more sulfur dioxide in a plume, the dimmer the ray that shines through.

When volcano detectives fly over a volcano, FLYSPEC measures the intensity of the special ray as it shines through a plume. Then it calculates the amount of sulfur dioxide present.

That's a lot of work for a tool smaller than bottle of sunscreen!

Soda Bottle Volcano

Make your own volcano out of a soda bottle. The bottom of the bottle represents a magma chamber. The narrow opening is like the vent. Your hand will clog the vent, like cooled, hardened magma. When you mix vinegar and baking soda you make carbon dioxide, the same gas volcanoes emit. Get ready to create your own gas explosion!

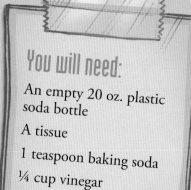

You will need:

An empty 20 oz. plastic soda bottle

A tissue

1 teaspoon baking soda

¼ cup vinegar

1. Spoon baking soda into a tissue, gather the sides of the tissue and twist it to form a narrow bundle. Pour vinegar into the soda bottle.

2. Go outside or somewhere you can make a mess. Holding the bottle away from people, push the baking soda bundle into the bottle and immediately cover the opening with your palm. Do you feel pressure? What do you hear?

3. Now make more gas! Still covering the opening, shake the bottle for 20 seconds. You should feel pressure build as the vinegar and baking soda mix to make more carbon dioxide. The hissing sound is similar to what you might hear near a real volcanic vent. Was the gas too powerful to hold back? What does that say about the power of gas under pressure? Take your hand off. Now do you see what makes volcanoes erupt?

4. Experiment with using more vinegar and baking soda. Can you make tissue pieces explode out of the bottle, like lava erupting explosively?

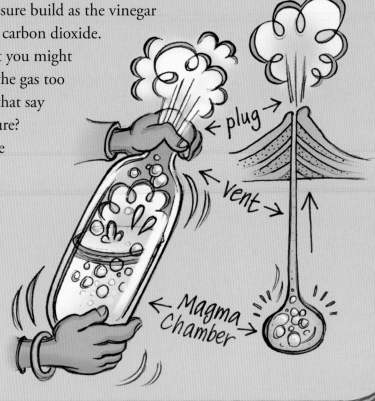

← plug →

← vent →

← Magma Chamber →

THE MYSTERY OF THE MISSING GAS

Ready to test your training on a second case? It's a tricky one.

As you know, on September 26, 2004, volcano detectives put Mount St. Helens on **Volcano Advisory, Code Yellow**. Earthquakes signaled that the volcano had awakened.

The very next day, Ken McGee hopped in a helicopter for his first gas search. "We found nothing," says Ken. "Big zeros."

Scientists wondered. Did the missing gas have something to do with the September rains? Maybe the gas was mixing with all that water underground so it couldn't escape.

But there was another more troubling explanation. "After days of earthquakes and no gas, we began to wonder whether the vent was plugged," says Ken. If the vent was plugged, magma and gases pushing to the surface are blocked, so pressure builds. "We worried about that," he says. "Really worried."

Then that night and early in the morning, shallow earthquakes increased to the rate of *four per minute.* "Things ramped up so high, we were getting magnitude 2s and 3s," says Seth Moran. "It was kind of ridiculous!"

But where was the gas? Was magma on the move or not? Was the gas being dissolved into water—or was it trapped, with pressure building?

The scientists debated raising the alert level to **Volcano Watch, Code Orange**. That would warn the public that the volcano was probably headed toward an eruption, but not immediately. Or they could go to the highest level: **Volcano Warning, Code Red**—eruption imminent!

What do you think?

SEARCH FOR THESE CLUES

☐ Carbon dioxide

☐ Hydrogen sulfide (rotten-egg smell)

☐ Sulfur dioxide (acrid burning smell)

CASE CLOSED

If you said to raise the alert level to **Volcano Watch, Code Orange**, you were right—at least as right as the volcano detectives. At 10:40 A.M. on September 29, scientists raised the alert level for Mount St. Helens. The notice read: "Explosions from the lava dome could occur suddenly and without further warning. Explosions would be expected to produce ash clouds that rise several thousand feet above the crater rim . . ."

The scientists put out their warning, and then they watched and waited.

All that day and the next, the earthquakes continued. The scientists took another gas search flight on the 30th. Zippo—no gas.

The surface of the volcano remained calm. Was the warning too early?

Then, at 11:57 A.M. on October 1, Mount St. Helens began to hiss. Tssssss! Steam and some ash shot 12,000 feet into the air for nearly thirty minutes. A seismic station was blown to bits.

This was exciting, but the investigation had only just begun. A true eruption only happens when magma reaches the surface. Detectives still didn't know if—or when—this would happen.

Time to gather more clues.

How Is an Eruption Like a Birthday?

A volcano rumbles with earthquakes. It shoots steam and ash into the air. Pretty cool fireworks, huh? But hold on—the explosion might not be an eruption. The word "eruption" actually means that new magma from underground has reached the surface. Once magma has erupted to the surface, scientists even give it a new name: lava! If new rock is born, Happy Birthday! It's an eruption!

chapter 3

DEFORMATION CLUES

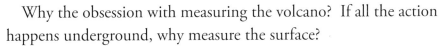

MAKING A MOUNTAIN OUT OF A MOLEHILL

When Mount St. Helens was a lovely, forested mountain, volcano detective Dan Dzurisin and his colleagues measured the slopes. After the top slid off in the 1980 eruption, he paced the steaming crater, clamoring over big boulders and scraping his elbows and knees, to measure it. Through the early 1980s, when lava oozed out into big pancake-shaped blobs, Dan visited the crater over and over to measure the growing dome.

Why the obsession with measuring the volcano? If all the action happens underground, why measure the surface?

Because it gives clues about what's happening beneath. "Imagine a mole tunneling under a lawn," says Dan. When the mole moves, the grass bumps up. "Magma moving underground does the same thing," he says. "It can actually lift the ground above it." When magma is close to the surface, the bulge it makes can grow hundreds of feet high and hundreds of feet wide!

WHERE'S THE MOLEHILL?

When magma is deeper underground, the changes are much smaller. Imagine a huge mole clawing its way up from five miles underground. The dirt the mole pushes up is spread over a large area, so it only raises the surface a little bit.

The same thing happens when magma moves deep within the Earth. "It will push up a large area, miles across, but just a tiny bit, less than you can even see," says Dan. This bulge deforms the ground, so volcano detectives look for deformation clues. Even less than an inch of swelling five miles from Mount St. Helens is a deformation clue that magma is on the move.

Adjusting a remote field camera

MEASURING A MOLEHILL

How can you tell if the ground for miles around has risen less than an inch? It's like trying to measure how much you've grown today. If you look at photos of yourself taken over the years, you can see yourself grow. Volcano detectives do the same thing. They fly above the crater and shoot special 3-D photos. The photos show the exact length, width, and height of every part of the volcano. Scientists compare photos taken at different times to see how the shape of the volcano changes.

But volcano detectives can't always shoot photos above an active volcano. So Dan relies on another amazing tool: GPS. Is that some kind of volcanic alphabet soup? Nah! GPS stands for Global Positioning System. The name actually says a lot—a GPS instrument reads signals from satellites orbiting the Earth to calculate your *exact position* anywhere on the *globe!*

"GPS is a real workhorse," says Dan. "It's so flexible. You can mount a GPS somewhere and see if that spot moves and by how much. You can carry it around and get exact positions at hundreds or thousands of places. We can even drop it into a crater to ride some erupting lava!"

Will Mount St. Helens erupt lava? Read on to find out.

placing a GPS unit

The Spider Surfs

The Itsy Bitsy Spider climbed up the volcanic wall! Well, not exactly. But the way scientists rigged up the GPS device to ride bulges in active volcanoes is pretty awesome.

Normally, detectives go to great lengths to attach the GPS to something solid, bolting or cementing it to a big rock outcrop. But when a volcano is active, no one wants to secure a GPS to a hunk of lava that could be blown up at any moment.

So a couple handy detectives thought: What if we stuck a GPS into a metal trunk? We could lower the trunk right into the crater…

"And it worked," says Dan Dzurisin with a laugh. "Except the trunk fell over in heavy wind."

But the scientists didn't give up. "Let's put legs on it!" they said.

So they built three legs for the trunk, for stability. And they dubbed their creation "The Spider." When dropped into a steaming volcanic crater, this Spider "surfs" the moving Earth. Kowabunga, dude!

Build a Bulge

See how magma pooling underground swells the land above it. The balloon is the magma chamber, your breath will be like the magma, and the straw is the vent.

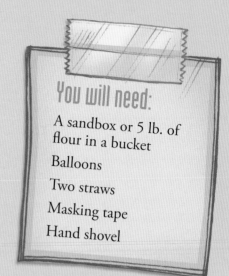

You will need:

A sandbox or 5 lb. of flour in a bucket

Balloons

Two straws

Masking tape

Hand shovel

1. Tape the straws together, end-to-end. Tape the mouth of the balloon over the end of one straw so it's airtight.

2. Dig a hole in the sand and bury the balloon so that one straw is buried and one sticks out. Smooth the sand.

3. Slowly inflate the balloon by blowing into the straw. How soon can you see cracks in the surface? Inflate the balloon until you think it's full. What does the sand look like now?

4. What would happen if all the magma erupted out of the magma chamber so fast that it couldn't be replaced from below? To see, blow up your balloon, cover the end of the straw with your thumb, and bury the balloon in the sand with the straw sticking up. Smooth the sand. Now release the air. What shape is the sand now? (This is called a caldera. Have you ever seen a photo of Crater Lake in Oregon? Now *that's* a crater!)

THE MYSTERY OF THE BULGE AND TREMOR

When Mount St. Helens rumbled to life in 2004, two volcano detectives flew above the crater to shoot some photos. They didn't see anything out of the ordinary.

But when Dan Dzurisin and others reviewed these photos later, they spotted something on the big chunk of ice that covers the crater floor. The glacier had three long cracks in the shape of a triangle. In the next few days, detectives flying over the crater saw a huge bulge cracking apart the 400-foot-deep glacier. "This monstrous bulge on the crater floor told me that the volcano was serious," says Dan.

The bump continued to grow. "We'd fly out there and say, 'Oh my goodness, it's bigger than yesterday!' It was growing so fast, you could see it with your naked eye!" says Dan. The bulge grew to the area of a football field and the height of a house!

Then on October 1, steam exploded from the edge of the bulge. The very next day, Mount St. Helens shot off another small steam explosion that lasted a couple of minutes. Gas detectives on the scene sniffed out only tiny amounts of gas: a little carbon dioxide, a whiff of hydrogen sulfide, and no sulfur dioxide.

"The ground surface was rising," says Dan, "The glacier was cracking and there were thousands of earthquakes. Magma had to be very near the surface. But still, there was very little gas. Was the magma explosive or not? We didn't know."

Then, something dramatic happened. The earthquakes shifted from small separate earthquakes to a continuous tremor that lasted fifty minutes. A harmonic tremor! That's a big clue that magma is on the move!

The scientists debated moving to **Volcano Warning, Code Red**, the highest alert level. It says an eruption—a serious, potentially violent eruption—is imminent. Johnston Ridge visitors' center might be evacuated, hiking trails closed, and airplanes diverted.

What do you think? Is an explosive eruption imminent? Should Mount St. Helens go **Volcano Warning, Code Red**?

SEARCH FOR THESE CLUES

- ☐ A bulge on the volcano
- ☐ Carbon dioxide, hydrogen sulfide, or sulfur dioxide
- ☐ A harmonic tremor

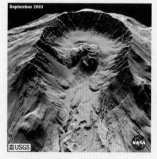
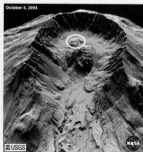

September 2003   October 2004

If you guessed that Mount St. Helens should go to **Warning, Code Red**, you're in good company. On October 2, 2004, the volcano detectives sounded the alarm. Johnston Ridge visitors' center closed. Commercial flights over the volcano were barred.

On October 3, another harmonic tremor lasting twenty-five minutes shook the mountain. The volcano detectives held their breath.

That night and the next day, the volcano shot out small jets of steam. Gas scientists detected tiny puffs of carbon dioxide and hydrogen sulfide, but still no sulfur dioxide. If a really humongous eruption was imminent, the detectives continued to wonder: where was the gas?

Then, on October 5, Mount St. Helens had its biggest steam and ash explosion since rumbling back to life. The blast lasted more than an hour, rose 12,000 feet in the air and dusted nearby towns with ash.

People all around the country were riveted. "But that's not what we meant by **Code Red**," says Seth Moran. "We were expecting something bigger, like a huge ash column shooting 40,000 feet in the air, sending searing-hot pyroclastic flows down the volcano."

But that didn't happen.

What was Mount St. Helens up to? Read on to delve deeper into this mystery.

chapter 4
HEAT CLUES

THE HEAT IS ON

Yowza! The inside of the Earth is hot. Scorching hot. Searing hot. Melt-metal-and-rock hot. And the deeper you go, the hotter it gets.

Even though it's hot inside the Earth, the surface of the planet is generally the same temperature as the air. Like your blanket keeping the heat in your bed, the Earth's crust, where we live, is a great insulator. Good thing or our shoes would melt when we walked!

Why, rookie, should you care that it's cool on the surface, but hot underground? It's simple: Volcanoes can't sneak magma to the Earth's surface without heating things up. A hot spot on the ground means . . . eruption!

TAKING A VOLCANO'S TEMPERATURE

Scientists have yet to develop a mile-long thermometer to stick down a volcano's vent. So heat detectives buzz over the crater in helicopters, shooting pictures. Shooting pictures? You mean you can see heat? Well, yes.

When you gaze at the glowing embers of a fire, you can see how heat makes light, and color. Some of the embers glow red, others orange, others yellow. Hot rock glows different colors at different temperatures, too. Rocks glowing orange to yellow are more than 1,650°F. Dark to bright cherry red rock is about 1,165°F, and a faint red glow can be seen in lava as cool as 895°F.

HOT SPOTS

Volcano detectives scout for spots in the crater that are hotter than normal. The larger the spot and the higher the temperature, the more likely the volcano is about to erupt.

So what's normal at Mount St. Helens? The crater is glacier country, home to a 400-foot thick hunk of ice and snow. The temperature there should be, well, freezing (32°F). When magma swells under such a huge glacier, you won't see temperatures shoot up to 1,000°F right away. You'll see melted ice.

But to our eyes, a 33°F spot looks just like one that is 200°F—neither one is hot enough to glow. So heat detectives use infrared cameras, which can detect much lower and higher temperatures and smaller changes in temperatures.

Using an infrared camera, volcano detectives might notice some spots in the crater that are slightly above freezing a week or so before an eruption. In the days right before an eruption, the temperatures might rise up to 212°F, the boiling point of water. Magma about to pop to the surface would really heat things up. You might see a rapidly growing hot spot that's 400, 500, even 1,000°F!

Infrared

Photo

Scientist Cynthia Gardner with **HOT** lava rocks →

SOME LIKE IT HOT

Detectives also use heat clues to try to deduce how the lava will behave when it erupts. Red, runny basaltic lava, which would flow peacefully out of the vent, is really hot—more than 2,000°F. Thicker lava, the type found in Mount St. Helens' crater, is a cooler 1,500°F. Lava thickens and eventually hardens when cooled, so temperatures under 1,000°F mean a cement-like lava or even solid rock could erupt.

That's fine if there's not much gas powering the eruption. Lava sludge or giant lava boulders would push out slowly, building back the mountaintop. But if gas is trapped in thick or solid lava, ouch! Those lava boulders—and the glacier—could be blown to bits and hurled sky-high, unleashing searing flows of ash and gas and triggering a catastrophic mudflow.

Volcanic Videogame

How would you like to get paid to play video games? Heat detective Jim Vallance does! To take heat pictures of Mount St. Helens, Jim mounts a Forward Looking Infrared Radiometer (FLIR) to the nose of a helicopter. FLIR is basically two cameras: a regular video camera and an infrared camera, which can see heat.

Inside the helicopter, Jim watches a video screen with a joystick in hand. As the helicopter flies, Jim scans the crater searching for heat, driving the cameras with the joystick. When Jim sees something interesting he points and shoots.

"It's just like a video game," says Jim. "You have to keep the camera steady while the pilot maneuvers the helicopter. The aircraft is moving all over the place, it's tilting, and you're trying to keep the camera on target. You're pushing the button, but instead of blowing up the bad guys, you're shooting photos of the crater!"

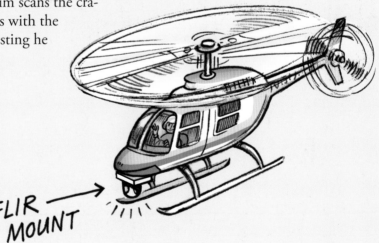

FLIR MOUNT

Lava Races

1. Different kinds of lava flow at different speeds. To see this, place a spoonful of syrup, cooking oil, and honey (your lava samples) side by side on one end of the cookie sheet. Tilt the tray—ready, set, go! How long does it take each kind of "lava" to race to the bottom of the tray?

2. The speed that lava flows is affected by how hot or cold it is. Fill two containers partway with syrup, two partway with cooking oil, and two partway with honey. Put one of each kind in the hot pot and cover it. Put the others in the freezer. Wait 5 minutes then repeat the race with the heated and cooled liquids.

You will need:

Six small, covered containers

Pancake syrup

Cooking oil

Honey

Freezer

Pot filled with hot water

Metal cookie sheet

Which of your "lavas" would flow out of a volcano the fastest? Which would be the slowest? How did temperature affect their runniness? Experiment with thicker foods, like butter, jelly, and chocolate. How might the shape of a volcano be affected by the temperature and runniness of the lava that erupts?

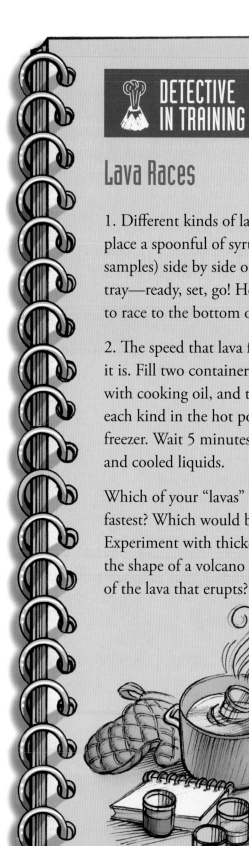
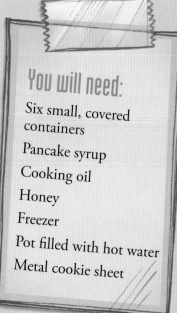

THE MYSTERY OF THE BOILING GLACIER

O.K., Detective-in-Training, put down the FLIR joystick and try your hand at this case.

What happens when you mix heaps of scorching rock with tons of ice and snow? Mudflow! Since the 1980 eruption, the glacier in Mount St. Helens' crater had grown to an average of 400 feet thick. That's enough ice to fill 40,000 swimming pools!

"From the beginning, we were concerned about really dramatic melting," says heat detective Jim Vallance. A volcano scattering hot rock can melt tons of ice. That water could create big mudflows that could race down the valley, burying people and houses.

Volcano detectives wanted to provide early warning of an eruption and any mudflow. So they needed to take the temperature of the bulging glacier.

During the first FLIR flight on October 1, 2004, the infrared detected little patches of heat, around 200°F. Six minutes later, Mount St. Helens spouted steam, right from the hot spot. "But we didn't see magmatic temperatures," says Jim. "Magma is ten times hotter."

Then, on October 4, Jim's colleague, Dave Schneider, found a new clue—a small boiling lake on the bulge. Maximum temperature of the area? 390°F!

In the next few days, clues came fast and furiously. But they were confusing. After the volcano's sixth steam and ash explosion on October 5, the earthquakes quieted down, to about one a minute with a top magnitude of only 1.0. Two days later, gas detective Ken McGee finally found his gas: tons of carbon dioxide, hydrogen sulfide, and sulfur dioxide! Magma was definitely behind the activity—and the gas was no longer trapped.

The bulge in the crater continued to grow. By October 10th, detectives noticed that the bulge had grown about 10 percent in just three days!

Jim Vallance noticed something else that day. The bubbling glacier lake had dried up. Heat had spread over a broader area—spanning 110 yards, about the length of a soccer field. "Where there used to be just little hot spots, we had this whole big area that had warmed up," says Jim. How warm? Up to 550°F!

Was magma about to break the surface? Would the lava be hot and runny? Sticky and explosive? Solid rock?

Would the bulge explode? What would happen to the glacier? What do you think?

SEARCH FOR THESE CLUES

☐ Temperature rising over 500°

☐ A large or growing hot spot

☐ Sulfur dioxide

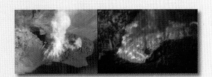

Photo   Infrared

CASE 4

CASE CLOSED

If you deduced that solid lava would erupt to the surface without exploding, you were right. Congratulations! You've predicted a real Mount St. Helens eruption and earned your detective badge!

On October 11, 2004, a huge pinkish-gray slab of solid magma, upright like a shark fin, shoved its way to the Earth's surface. Mount St. Helens was officially erupting for the first time in eighteen years!

The lava slab was hot—around 900°F. But not hot enough to be liquid. The lava erupted as solid rock and just shoved the glacier aside.

The clues gave Mount St. Helens away all along. Earthquakes told detectives that magma was on the move. The bulge was solid evidence that magma was near the surface. Elevated temperatures suggested the volcano would erupt, but probably with thick or solid lava. "And gases told us the true story," says Ken McGee. "That this wasn't going to be an explosive eruption. There just wasn't enough gas."

But there *was* enough gas to push magma from miles underground to the surface.

Lava began erupting freely—pumping truckloads of brand new rock into the crater every single second. Within five months, Mount St. Helen's new dome rose 550 feet. The dome could cover sixty city blocks with buildings more than thirty stories high. Mount St. Helens was growing back!

Read on to predict how long the eruption will last, and whether we'll see red, hot runny lava—or something really explosive!

chapter 5
LAVA CLUES

ROCK AND ROLL

"When a volcano erupts, I can't wait to get my hands on some fresh lava," says geologist John Pallister. That's because when a volcano erupts lava, it's like a criminal leaving a wallet at the crime scene. Lava rocks hold all kinds of clues about what happened to the magma underground—and what the volcano might be up to next.

How do volcano detectives gather lava clues? "You can answer the most important questions simply by looking at a rock sample," says John.

LAVA LESSONS

First question: Is there gas stuck in the lava? If lava has a lot of trapped gas, that's ammo for an explosion. "To figure out if a rock is gas-rich, you hold it in your hand," says John. "Is it dense, solid rock? Or lightweight and puffed up, full of bubbles?" Dense and heavy rocks have less gas. Light, puffy rocks are filled with gas. Some lava, called pumice, is so gas-filled and lightweight it can actually float on water!

Pumice

Now lean in for a close look. Does the rock have shiny bits of glass in it? Glassy shards are gas bubbles in the magma that cooled quickly and turned to glass.

THE COLOR OF DANGER

Volcano detectives also want to know what kind of lava they're dealing with. The color is a dead giveaway: Is the rock sample black, gray, or white? The hot runny lava that pours out of Hawaiian volcanoes turns into dark rock when it hardens, called basalt. Everyone sighs with relief if they see basalt. Liquid basalt generally releases its gas without exploding.

Gray rock, called andesite, is thicker, and can be explosive if it's filled with gas. Light gray or white rock is most likely dacite. Dacite is very thick. If it's filled with gas, an eruption can be very explosive indeed.

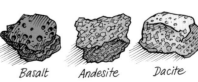

Basalt   Andesite   Dacite

CLOCK THAT ROCK

Volcano detectives also look to lava to retrace the magma's steps. How fast did the magma shoot up the soda straw?

"The speed of the ascent matters a lot," says John. A slower moving magma has time to release trapped gases safely. Magma that erupts more quickly can also erupt more explosively. Bammo!

Does lava have a speedometer? It sure does—the texture of a lava sample reveals the story. Magma that rises really fast cools quickly and solidifies to glass. If a lava sample is smooth and shiny or has smooth glassy chunks, it rose and cooled quickly.

A slower rising magma has time to form crystals, which are solid, separate chunks inside the rock. Bumpy, gritty rock full of crystals took its sweet time reaching the surface. The bigger the crystals, the slower the magma rose and cooled.

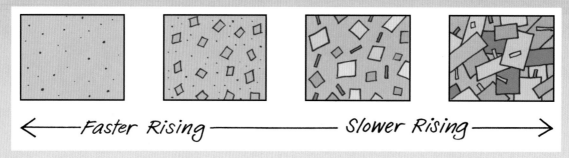

← Faster Rising — Slower Rising →

ROCKIN' RECIPE

Once you've gathered your lava clues, put all the information together. If your lava sample is thick lava, full of gas, and fast rising, get back. Way back. This volcano is a powder keg ready to really blow.

The Making of Jaws

When Mount St. Helens began erupting lava, John Pallister was eager for a sample. But not so eager that he wanted to risk getting blown up. "We were scratching our heads about how to get lava samples from the crater," he says.

The detectives needed a way to collect rocks while hovering in a helicopter. John surfed the Web for ideas.

He found a 1958 photograph from a deep-sea expedition. The photo showed a big steel dredge. He took the picture to a machine shop and asked, "Can you build me something like this?"

The machinist built a huge metal shovel with teeth. "We rigged a steel cable onto a helicopter and clamped the dredge onto it," says John. From the cockpit, the pilot lowered the dredge to the crater floor, near the vent, and dragged it along the surface. Presto! It filled with lava rocks!

But what should they call the contraption? The inspiration came from the deep sea. The tool had an impressive set of chompers. So John named his creation after the famous movie-star shark, "Jaws." Duh, duh. Duh, duh. Duh, duh!

steel 'jaws'

lava rocks

wire mesh collecting bag

Lickable Lava

In this activity you'll see how different rates of cooling affect the formation of crystals in a rock—a candy rock.

1. Grease a baking sheet and put it in the freezer to chill. With an adult's help, cook ½ cup sugar in a saucepan over medium heat. This syrup is your magma. When it's completely melted, pour it on the frozen baking sheet. Put the sheet back in the freezer. This represents magma that cools quickly. After 5 minutes, take the sheet out and look at the smooth, glassy sugar.

2. With an adult's help, heat 1 cup of sugar and ½ cup water in a saucepan, stirring until the sugar dissolves and the mixture boils. Stop stirring and let the mixture boil for one minute. Have the adult pour the syrup into a glass with the Popsicle stick in it. Storing it at room temperature lets it cool slowly.

3. Check it every few days. How do the crystals forming slowly on the stick compare with the crystals that cooled quickly in the freezer? Now you can eat your experiment. You've made lava you can lick!

You will need:
- An adult to help
- Baking sheet
- Sugar
- Water
- Saucepan
- Stove and freezer
- A glass
- A Popsicle stick

THE MYSTERY OF THE DISAPPEARING GLASS SHARDS

When Mount St. Helens finally erupted lava on October 11, 2004, John Pallister got excited. "We all wanted to know what had erupted," says John. "Dacite, andesite, or basalt?"

When John held the first warm lava rock in his hand, he could tell by its whitish-gray color that it was dacite, the thickest of the three magma types found at Mount St. Helens. Lacking bubbles or glass shards, the lava held very little gas, so it was heavy.

"The texture felt sugary, granular, full of tiny crystals," he recalls. John guessed that the magma had cooled at shallow levels, becoming rock solid near the surface. "Most likely this was magma left over from the 1980s," he says. That meant it was old, stale, and flat—the way a soda goes flat when you leave it open.

But still, he wondered, "What was fueling this eruption? If there's no gas, what's pushing out this incredible heap of solid rock?" Yes, a heap. Soon after Mount St. Helens blasted its way through the vent, it was cranking out lava in heaps. About a dump truck load every second!

For the first few weeks of the eruption, John grabbed lava samples by dragging Jaws up the sides of the enormous, growing dome.

But he wasn't sure he was snagging samples of *new* lava. So in early November, he landed in the helicopter near the steaming new dome. "It was exciting," he says. "I grabbed my gloves, my gas mask, a pick ax, two buckets, and some fiberglass insulation. I figured if I picked up glowing rocks, I couldn't just put them on the floor of the helicopter or they'd melt right through!"

John jumped out of the helicopter. "It was snow and ice and rubbly and bouldery. But I scrambled up this steep slope with my pick ax and my buckets, running as fast as I could. The dome was steaming but I got up there and started shoveling hunks out. Then I did my best to run back down without spilling my bucket, jumped in the helicopter, and away we went."

At first glance, the lava he collected resembled early samples: whitish-gray, heavy, with small crystals. But a few rocks held a surprise. "We got small fragments that were unlike the rest—dark, glassy fragments," he says. These samples rose too fast to crystallize and turn whitish-gray.

The detectives wondered: *Would the eruption continue? Did the glassy fragments mean a new batch of deep, possibly gas-rich magma was surging up? Would this eruption turn explosive? What do you think?*

SEARCH FOR THESE CLUES

- ☐ Weight of the lava rock
- ☐ Color of the lava
- ☐ Crystals in the lava

DEPARTMENT of VOLCANIC INVESTIGATION

	SENT	REC'D

OFFICIAL BUSINESS:

If you predicted that Mount St. Helens would continue to erupt massive amounts of lava for a long, long time, you were right! After the first few months, the eruption of lava slowed slightly from a dump-truck load every second to a pickup-truck load every second. This is still fast enough to fill your bedroom with lava in less than a minute—and rebuild Mount St. Helens to its pre-1980 glory of 9,677 feet in your lifetime!

If you predicted that this eruption would last, you out-sleuthed most of the volcano detectives. Seth Moran, the earthquake detective, has predicted, time and again, that the eruption would soon be over. "I kept making the statement, 'It looks like it's really done now!'" he says. But it just keeps going.

And Seth's not alone. "I've been thinking for months now that this eruption is going to stop because the gas is so low," says gas detective Ken McGee. "But who knows, it could last five more months or five more years. It could fill up the entire crater." He pauses, then says, "Eventually it will, whether it's this eruption or the next one. It will."

Dan Dzurisin and Jim Vallance and the other detectives wonder if there's new magma or gas fueling the eruption from below. "How could it just keep erupting if there's not something down there driving it?" Jim asks.

That's why John Pallister regularly scrapes out new chunks of lava to study. Why Jim Vallance aims his heat-sensing joystick at the vent and shoots infrared photos. Why Dan Dzurisin watches Mount St. Helens change shape. Why Ken McGee flies overhead sucking up gas samples. Why Seth Moran listens to the seismographs on Mount St. Helens sing.

They're all looking for clues that new magma is going to dramatically change the course of this eruption. "We could see thick molten rock," says John Pallister. "We could get explosive eruptions. We could even get basalt lava, with spectacular red, runny lava falls oozing down. At this volcano, anything can happen."

The mysteries of Mount St. Helens never end.

Your job, Volcano Detective, has just begun.

CAUTION: EXPLOSIVE SUBJECT MATTER   No 06892734C

MOUNT ST. HELENS TODAY

When this book went to press, Mount St. Helens was still erupting. Even if this eruption stops, the volcano *will* rumble to life again. Mount St. Helens will rebuild to its former majesty—and it will blow its top again. It's only a matter of time. To see what Mount St. Helens is up to now—and to find the latest clues—visit the author's website at www.elizabethrusch.com.

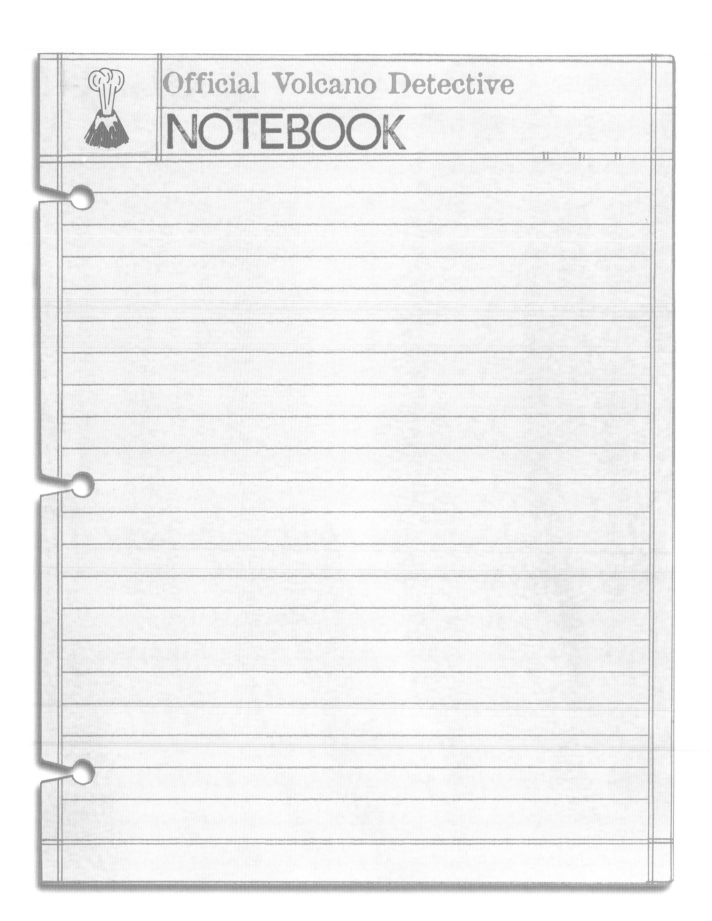

Official Volcano Detective
NOTEBOOK

VOCABULARY

ANDESITE: A gray to black volcanic rock. Andesitic lava can erupt explosively.

ASH: Tiny bits of blasted volcanic rock.

BASALT: A hard, black volcanic rock. Basaltic lava often erupts fluidly.

BULGE: A bump on a volcano formed when magma pushes up to just under the surface.

CALDERA: A large pit or crater formed when a volcano collapses into its magma chamber.

CARBON DIOXIDE: CO_2. An invisible, odorless volcanic gas. Except for water vapor, it is the most abundant gas released by volcanoes.

CORE: The extremely hot region in the center of the Earth.

CRATER: A deep bowl formed by either an explosion or a collapse of a volcano.

CRUST: The Earth's outermost layer.

CRYSTAL: A solid mineral that forms when certain liquids cool slowly.

DACITE: A light gray volcanic rock that can erupt very explosively.

DEFORMATION: A change in the surface of a volcano or the area surrounding it caused by magma moving underground.

DOME: A mound or pile of thick lava that can grow large and steep.

DORMANT: A volcano that has not erupted for a long time but may erupt in the future.

EARTHQUAKE SWARM: A group of earthquakes happening in the same place, one after another.

ERUPTION: When magma from under a volcano reaches the Earth's surface.

GEOLOGIST: A scientist who studies the Earth.

GPS: Global Positioning System. A tool that can pinpoint an exact location using satellite signals.

HARMONIC TREMOR: Continuous, rhythmic earthquakes that often happen before or during volcanic eruptions.

HYDROGEN SULFIDE: H_2S. A gas with a rotten egg smell. A volcano may emit hydrogen sulfide when the volcanic gas sulfur dioxide mixes with hot water.

INFRARED CAMERA: A tool that measures temperature by photographing heat radiation.

LAHAR: An Indonesian term for mudflow.

LANDSLIDE: A large mass of earth falling or sliding rapidly under the force of gravity.

LAVA: Magma that has erupted to the surface. May be liquid or cooled to a solid rock.

MAGMA: Melted or partially melted rock and gases beneath the Earth's surface.

MAGMA CHAMBER: An area of melted or partially melted rock and gases beneath a volcano.

MAGNITUDE: A number that represents the power of an earthquake.

MANTLE: The soft, hot part of the inside of the Earth between the core and the crust.

MUDFLOW: A thick mixture of water, ash, and lava that is pulled down by gravity. Also called a lahar or debris flow.

PLATES: Massive slabs of the Earth's surface. Many volcanoes occur around the edges of plates.

PLUME: A cloud of water vapor, volcanic gases, and/or volcanic ash that can rise from a volcanic vent.

PUMICE: A light-colored volcanic rock so filled with gas bubbles that it may float on water.

PYROCLASTIC FLOW: Hot volcanic gases and ash that can tumble down a volcano.

SEISMOGRAPH: A tool that measures ground vibrations, especially from earthquakes.

SULFUR DIOXIDE: SO_2. A volcanic gas. When sulfur dioxide combines with water in your mouth, it forms sulfuric acid, giving you an acrid or acidic taste.

VENT: An opening in a volcano through which lava, ash, and gas can erupt.

READ MORE

ADAMS, SIMON. *The Best Book of Volcanoes.* New York, NY: Kingfisher, 2001.

BLOBAUM, CINDY. *Geology Rocks!* Charlotte, VT: Williamson, 1999.

HICKSON, CATHERINE. *Mt. St. Helens: Surviving the Stone Wind.* Vancouver, BC: Tricouni Press, 2005.

LAUBER, PATRICIA. *Volcano: The Eruption and Healing of Mt. St. Helens.* New York, NY: Aladdin, 1986.

LINDOP, LAURIE. *Probing Volcanoes.* Brookfield, CT: Millbrook Press, 2003.

O'BRIEN-PALMER, MICHELLE. *How the Earth Works.* Chicago, IL: Chicago Review Press, 2002.

ROBSON, PAM. *Mountains and Our Moving Earth.* Brookfield, CT: Copper Beech Books, 2001.

THOMPSON, DICK. *Volcano Cowboys: The Rocky Evolution of a Dangerous Science.* New York, NY: St. Martin's Press, 2000.

SURF MORE

Annenberg Media
Can We Predict Volcanic Eruptions?
www.learner.org/exhibits/volcanoes/

Cascades Volcano Observatory
http://vulcan.wr.usgs.gov/

Mount St. Helens VolcanoCam
www.fs.fed.us/gpnf/volcanocams/msh/

Smithsonian Global Volcanism Program
www.volcano.si.edu/index.cfm

USGS Volcano Hazards Program
http://volcanoes.usgs.gov

Special Thanks

When I began the research for this book, I discovered that little has been published on the current eruption or on the cutting-edge science of volcano monitoring. This book, truly, would not have been possible without the time and expertise of the following scientists at the USGS Cascades Volcano Observatory in Vancouver, Washington: Dan Dzurisin, Ken McGee, Seth Moran, John Pallister, and Jim Vallance.

Special thanks to USGS scientists Carolyn Driedger and Cynthia Gardner and to my editor Gary Luke for helping me find a way to shape the information and tell this story.

Thanks, too, to everyone (especially the kids) who commented on drafts: Jim Adams, Carson Brindle, Mike Clynne, Lisa Cohn, Gavin Leach, Michelle McCann, Sue Moshofsky, Katie O'Dell, Rachel Osmundsen, Catherine Paglin, Mary Rehmann, Clara Rehmann, Simone Riley, Craig Rusch, Katrina Swope, Trevor Swope, Cara Scalpone, Sam Zasloff-Cohen, and Stephen Brand's students at Chapman Elementary School in Portland, Oregon. Addie Boswell, thank you for your stellar research, editing and transcribing.

Finally, thanks to my son Cobi, whose eyes practically popped out of his head when a ranger handed him a piece of just-erupted Mount St. Helens lava. Your fascination inspired the book.

—*Elizabeth Rusch*

About the Author

CRAIG RUSCH

When Elizabeth Rusch was 13, she was glued to the television in her home in Connecticut watching the 1980 eruption of Mount St. Helens. At the time, she didn't even know that the United States had any active volcanoes. She knows better now. A long-time resident of Portland, Oregon, Rusch can see Mount St. Helens and three other Cascade volcanoes from her neighborhood.

Rusch's award-winning writing has been published in dozens of national magazines and newspapers for adults and children, including *Backpacker, Mother Jones, Harper's, Parenting, American Girl, Colorado Kids,* and the *Oregonian.* Her first children's book, *Generation Fix,* was a *Smithsonian* magazine Notable Children's Book and a finalist for the International Reading Association's Children's Book Award and the Oregon Book Award. She thinks Mount St. Helens should get an award for the Coolest American Volcano.

About the Illustrator

Illustrator K.E. Lewis grew up in the Pacific Northwest, and remembers camping on the banks of Spirit Lake and climbing through old lava tubes near Mount St Helens with her middle school classmates a few years before the 1980 eruption.

She lives in Seattle, where she shares her art studio with three cockatiels and a pair of gerbils. They keep an eye on their nearest Cascades volcano, Mount Rainier.